# Sex Coupons for Wife

having sex once in the location of your choosing

not leaving you one time

one day of no farting

one shower together where you get the water

oral sex session while
you're on your smart device

one day of no interruptions

one _____ with someone else

foot massage

sex movie of your choice

champagne in bed

one butt massage

fully body massage

3 kisses... at location of your choice

5 minute passionate kiss

chocolate body paint session

let's play doctors and nurses

Kama Sutra random page

a sensual massage

neck and shoulder massage

recreate your first dinner date together

spend a whole day in bed

night where you get to spread out on the bed

listen to each other's favorite love songs

tell each other a sex secret

write a love or sex letter or poem

write down 10 sex things
I love about you

one knock me off my feet kiss

night of role playing

one wild fantasy fulfilled sex

dress up night- you pick the outfit

pick something to lick off me

time where i have to admit "I'm wrong"

spur of the moment 69
followed by sex

romantic sex night in

1 hour oral sex

any position of choice

sex under the stars

one toy of choice

roleplay encounter of choice

sexy photo shoot
(if you'd be comfortable with that)

purchase of one toy of her choice

make dessert of your partner –
whipped cream, chocolate, cherries, etc.

thing that you want me to say (or not say) during sex

do what you want with Ice

night where you get the house all to yourself

day In which i get the hair out of the tub/shower

being forced to hear you tell that same story again

one post sex snack

21794383R00058

Made in the USA
San Bernardino, CA
05 January 2019